# Seals

## Victoria Blakemore

vblakemore.author@gmail.com

Copyright info/picture credits

Cover, wim claes/Shutterstock; Page 3, werner22brigitte/Pixabay; Page 5, skeeze/Pixabay; Page 7, skeeze/Pixabay; Page 9, flodambricourt/Pixabay; Pages 10-11, Patrick Poendl/AdobeStock; Page 13, christels/Pixabay; Page 15, elvis santa-na/AdobeStock; Page 17, WaltiGoehner/Pixabay; Page 19, kichigin19/AdobeStock; Page 21, skeeze /Pixabay; Page 23; skeeze /Pixabay; Page 25, Tim_Tonic/Pixabay; Page 27, A_Different_Perspective/Pixabay; Page 29, A_Different_Perspective/Pixabay; Page 31, Letti-S/Pixabay; Page 33, wim claes/Shutterstock

# Table of Contents

# What Are Seals?

Seals are a special kind of mammal called a pinniped. This means that they have flippers instead of feet. Other pinnipeds include sea lions and walruses.

There are about nineteen different kinds of seals. They differ in where they live, their size, and coloration.

Seals are **semi-aquatic**

mammals. They spend a lot of

time on land and in the water.

# Size

Seals can weigh from 100 to over 8,000 pounds, depending on the kind of seal.

The smallest kind of seal is the ringed seal. It grows to be about five feet long. The elephant seal is the largest. It can be up to twenty feet long.

Male seals are often larger than

female seals, but not always.

# Physical Characteristics

Seals have flippers. Their

flippers are webbed, which

allows them to move quickly

in the water.

All seals have fur, but most

only have a very short coat.

Their fur is covered with an oil

that helps to keep it

**waterproof.**

They have a thick layer of fat, called **blubber**, that helps to keep them warm in the cold waters.

# Habitat

Seals are found in arctic habitats. They are usually seen along the shoreline or in **coastal** waters.

They need to be very close to the water so that they can hunt their prey. They also need land so they can rest and warm up.

# Range

Most seals are found in the
Arctic circle or around
Antarctica.

They are often seen in countries
like Russia, Norway, Canada,
and the United States.

# Diet

Like other pinnipeds, seals are **carnivores**. They eat only meat.

Their diet is made up of fish, shellfish, and squid. Since their prey is all found in the ocean, seals must dive and swim to catch their prey.

Seals have whiskers that help them to sense movement. This helps them to find their prey when they are hunting.

Since seals eat prey that is small, they don't need to bite or chew. They often swallow their prey whole.

Seals rarely need to drink any water. They get most of the water they need from the food that they eat.

Predators like orcas hunt for seals

and sea lions. They can hunt

them out in the water or close to

shore.

# Communication

Seals use sound and movement to communicate. They make sounds like groans, growls, and whistles.

Harbor seals slap the water with their flippers if they are upset. Elephant seals rise up and make loud noises if they want to fight with other seals.

Seals can make noises

above and under the water.

# Movement

Seals are not very fast when they are on land. Their size and flippers make it difficult for them to move quickly.

In the water, seals are much faster. The shape of their body helps them to move quickly through the water. Their flippers help to **propel** them.

Seals can stay underwater

longer than many other

mammals. Harbor seals can stay

under for up to thirty minutes.

# Seal Pups

Mother seals usually have one baby, called a pup. Pups are born on land and learn to recognize their mother by a special call that she makes.

The mother can tell her baby from other pups by a special scent that pups have.

Seal pups grow very quickly and are able to go hunting with their mother after a few months.

# Seal Life

Seals live together in groups.

These groups are called pods

or rookeries. There can be

hundreds of seals in a rookery.


Rookeries hunt together. They

also help to watch out for

predators. When they aren't

hunting, they often nap in the

sun.

Some seals **molt**. They shed lots of their fur each year. When this happens, they stay on land where it is warmer.

# Staying Warm

Seals usually live where it is very cold. They have a few different ways to stay warm.

Their thick layer of **blubber** helps to keep them warm in the water. They also spend a lot of time laying in the sun.

Seals raise their flippers and tail fins out of the water to **absorb** heat from the sun. This is called rafting.

# Population

Some kinds of seals are **endangered**. There are not many left in the wild. Others are **vulnerable**. Many seal populations are **declining**.

Since seals are often in the water, it is impossible to know exactly how many are left in the wild.

Seal **lifespans** can **vary**. They can be between fifteen and forty years in the wild.

# Seals in Danger

Seals are facing many threats in the wild. Rising temperatures are causing ice to melt, which can affect seal habitats.

**Pollution** caused by humans can make seals sick or hurt. They are also hunted by people for their fur, skin, and meat.

Some **parasites** and other diseases are also making seals sick.

# Helping Seals

There are places around the world that help seals that are sick or hurt. They work to help seals get better so they can be released back into the wild.

In some places, there are laws that protect seals in the wild. They make it **illegal** for seals to be hunted by humans.

Temperatures in the Arctic have been getting warmer. This is causing ice to melt, which is not good for seals.

There are groups that are trying to help seals. They want to try to stop the change in temperature so that seal habitats are not destroyed.

# Glossary

**Absorb:** to take in or soak up

**Blubber:** the layer of fat under the skin of whales, seals, and sea mammals

**Carnivore:** an animal that eats only meat

**Coastal:** near a coast

**Declining:** getting smaller

**Endangered:** at risk of becoming extinct

**Illegal:** against the law

**Lifespan:** how long an animal lives

**Molt:** to shed skin, feathers, or fur

**Parasite:** a plant or animal that feeds off of other creatures

**Pollution**: poisons or wastes from human activities

**Propel**: to push forward

**Semi-aquatic**: an animal that lives on land and in the water

**Vary:** to change

**Vulnerable:** when an animal may become endangered if the population declines

**Waterproof:** not letting water through

# About the Author

Victoria Blakemore is a first grade

teacher in Southwest Florida with a

passion for reading.

You can visit her at

www.elementaryexplorers.com

# Also in This Series

| | | | | | | |
|---|---|---|---|---|---|---|
| Gray Wolves | Sloths | Flamingos | Camels | Koalas | Honey Bees | Pandas |
| Pangolins | White-Tailed Deer | Orcas | Giraffes | Corn | Meerkats | Echidnas |
| Walruses | Raccoons | Bald Eagles | Apples | Arctic Foxes | Red Pandas | Cassowaries |
| Tigers | Ladybugs | Moose | Beluga Whales | Leopards | Elephants | Jellyfish |
| Binturongs | Lions | Dolphins | Reindeer | Hammerhead Sharks | Hippos | Pumpkins |
| Peafowl | Chameleons | Florida Panthers | Aye-Ayes | Black Bears | Cheetahs | Manatees |
| Gingerbread | Polar Bears | Hot Chocolate | Orangutans | Coyotes | Marshmallows | Strawberries |

Victoria Blakemore

# Also in This Series

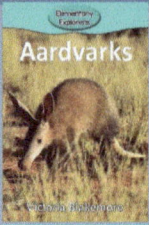

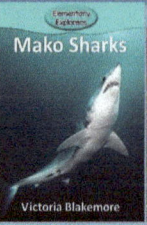

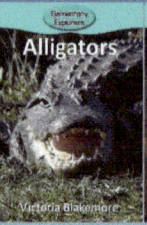

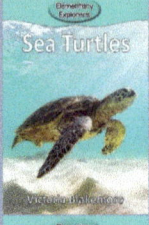

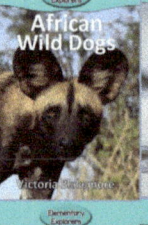

| | | | | | | |
|---|---|---|---|---|---|---|
| Aardvarks | Mako Sharks | Alligators | Frogs | Hedgehogs | Brown Bears | Bongos |
| Sea Turtles | Quokkas | Muskrats | Zebras | Red Foxes | Ring-Tailed Lemurs | Platypuses |
| Anteaters | Kangaroos | Rhinos | Jaguars | Wombats | Capybaras | Gorillas |
| Cats | Skunks | Butterflies | Dingoes | Snow Leopards | African Wild Dogs | Penguins |
| Whale Sharks | Wolverines | Warthogs | Caracals | Badgers | Seals | Hummingbirds |

Victoria Blakemore

www.ingramcontent.com/pod-product-compliance
Lightning Source LLC
Chambersburg PA
CBHW051253020426
42333CB00025B/3197